The Maine Dictionary

John McDonald

Illustrations by

Peter Wallace

Commonwealth Editions

Beverly, Massachusetts

To Joshua, Rebecca and Jeremiah, who have always listened
and laughed above and beyond the call . . .

Text copyright © 2000 by John McDonald

Illustrations copyright © 2000 by Peter Wallace

Commonwealth Editions

is an imprint of Memoirs Unlimited, Inc.,

266 Cabot Street, Beverly, Massachusetts 01915.

Visit us on the Web at: www.commonwealtheditions.com

ISBN 978-1-933212-69-2

10 9 8 7 6 5

INTRODUCTION

When the idea of publishing a Maine dictionary was born I'm not sure where I was. I was probably in the lower field by the brook cutting pucker brush (which see), and no one even bothered to call me. Not only was I absent from the delivery room—or "birthing room" as it's called these days—I wasn't even in the waiting room passing out big, smelly cigars. All I know is, I don't remember a thing about when the idea for this dictionary was born.

The thing I do remember is one day out of the blue I get a phone call from this editor from Massachusetts who starts off by saying, "John, we're thinking of doing a Maine dictionary and after looking around we think you're the guy to do it for us."

All business, I said professionally, "Say what?"

He explained that they had already had great success with a Boston dictionary and were looking to keep the success rolling with a dictionary of Maine words and phrases. He said he had read several of my newspaper columns, and despite that he still thought I could probably pound out the Maine dictionary he was looking to publish

After responding that I was flattered and would definitely consider the project I hung up the phone here at Storyteller Central and thought, "So much for cutting pucker brush. I've got to make me a pot of coffee and think about this."

Sure, I had used dictionaries from time to time throughout my life. But here was a publisher asking me to write one of the things. Two questions immediately came to mind:

1. Could I really write a dictionary? and
2. What do you think they put in the water down there in Massachusetts?

The thing that made all this a deadly serious matter was the fact that this dictionary I was being asked to write was supposed to be "funny." If I've learned one thing over the years it's that there's no more grim a task than trying to be comical.

At this stage—in a funny way—I didn't have a clue as to how I would write something that could be called *The Maine Dictionary*. I did know that people who wrote things like dictionaries were called "lexicographers" and that didn't bother me: I'd been called a lot worse.

After several days in this thinking mode I finally decided that if I was going to write a dictionary I should probably get out of the house and do stuff like "field recordings" and "research." I wasn't really sure what a "field recording" was, but I had read somewhere about writers going to remote picturesque places and making "field recordings." So I decided that was what I should do.

By the way, if you've ever tried to record a typical field, you know it's not as easy as it sounds. I learned that right off quick. Fact is, in my back field there's hardly any sound at all. And the sounds my field makes aren't the kind of sounds I thought of putting in either a field recording or a humorous dictionary.

After a few days of that taping foolishness I decided to take a trip Down East. I figured if I was going to be defining Maine words I'd better take a refresher course on how some of those words are still being used.

At one point I found myself sitting at the counter of a Down East diner (see *Dinah*) with a pad in one hand and a coffee (see *Coffey*) in the other. I began writing down words that people all around me were using.

Some of the customers would occasionally turn and look at me kind of funny, but I didn't care because I was a budding "lexicographer" working on a Maine dictionary and there was all kinds of work I had to do—like figuring out exactly what kind of work a lexicographer did.

Incidentally, I've noticed that ever since I started referring to myself as a lexicographer in general conversation I get some funny looks from some people, but I've also noticed that my throat is nowhere near as congested as it was when I started.

We could go on and on about all the exhaustive research that went into this book, but we know how few people out there read introductions. Most of us look at intros and say, "I'm sure looking forward to reading all this 'intro' garbage. Yeah, right."

Let's just say I awoke every morning by 5:00 and was at my computer by 5:20 and usually got my first sentence of the day done by 8:00 or 9:00. Using that method, and a lot of others that are too painful at this time to recall, I eventually got the book done.

It is to be expected that some sensitive individuals with finely tuned ears will peruse this work and then sincerely question the way certain words are rendered phonetically and defined here, which is as it should be.

To those discerning readers we say, "Oh, yeah, barnacle breath. Let's see you write one."

Other thoughtful readers will ask, "Hey, John, who appointed you an expert on Maine usage and speech patterns?"

To those kind readers we cordially answer: "Your muthah" (which see).

To some out-of-state critics—who claim to be speech experts but who's idea of Down East is really East 11th Street between Avenues C & D—we say: "Don't criticize us until you have walked with us through the aisles of Reny's in Rockland and really listened."

There are a lot of people I should probably thank at this point—like all those folks through the centuries who have contributed to Maine's colorful way with words—but at the risk of leaving one or two out I've decided to name only the most significant contributors to this dictionary.

A thank-you must also go out to my colleagues in the storytelling community. You know who you are—and what you've done.

—John McDonald

The Maine Dictionary

A

Aahx To inquiah of someone. For example, a tourist might aahx, "I'm heading for Meddybemps and was wondering if it made any difference which way I go here at this fork in the road?" And the Maineah would ansah, "Not to me, it don't, deah."

A'dultree Without going into gory details, let's just say in Maine getting caught in this is like a Florida hurricane or a Kansas tornado: in all three cases some poor fella's gonna lose his trailah.

Aegrahvate Something tourists sometimes do to natives, specially tourists who come up here to Maine to get away from it all but manage to bring it all with them in their 48-foot Winnebago towing a Jeep Grand Cherokee. A Mainer once said, "I have always found there is nuthin' wrong with a tourist that a little common sense and reasoning wunt aegrahvate."

Aeksent Funny way of talkin that most folks from away seem to have. Their aeksent can sometimes be so strong and their speech so distahted you can hahdly understand a wurd that comes out-uv-um.

Ahht Stuff that's promoted and supported by the Ahhts C'mmishn up there in 'gusta. Also, main product in places like Ogunquit and Munheg'n durin' the summah and hauled off in carloads by tourists.

Ankah Clevah nautical decoration seen on many arms and in front of almost every seafood restaurant.

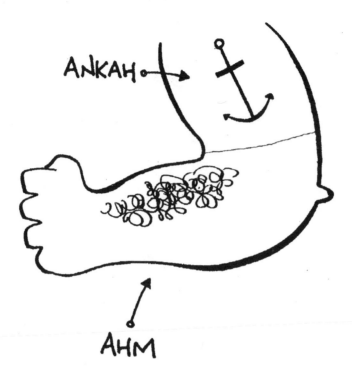

ANKAH

AHM

Ahm One of the only body pahts of a Mainah that should evah have a sun tan. And even then the tan should only cover ya left ahm—the one that's out the window of ya pickup—and the tan line has got to end just above the elbow. If you see someone with a tan clear to their shoulder or mowa, mistah, you're looking at a sun-wershipah, not a Mainah.

Ahndray the Seal Maine's other official state seal. André is no longer flipping his fins in this life but has gone to that great seal harbor in the sky. While alive he summered in Rockport and wintered at the Boston Aquarium.

AHNDRAY THE SEAL

André became a genuine media celebrity and the subject of much gossip as well as numerous books, films and interviews. A survey back in the 1980s showed André had better name recognition than Joseph Brennan, who happened to be governor of Maine at the time. If André were alive today, we have no doubt he would have his own show on cable and would be a frequent guest on Nightline whenever the subject at hand had anything to do with the coast of Maine or fish or New England celebrities. The closest thing we have these days to André would be the famed horror writer Steven King of Bangor. But he refuses to catch a fish in midair while clapping his hands on cue. They just don't make celebrities like Andre anymore.

Ahnt Ahnts are creatures that crawl on your kitchen counter or on your sandwiches at a picnic. Also used to describe the chocolate bits you sprinkle on top of ice cream cones. Another word for these is sprills. A few years back some summah complaints from Mahhsachusetts introduced the word "jimmies" to Maine in place of ahnts or sprills. Our ice cream cones haven't been the same since. Neither has much else here in Maine, come to think of it.

Akah In the rest of the country it's 43,560 square feet of land—but most Mainahs think such foolish numbers are some out-a-state lawyah's idea. Down East, where there's plenty of land, folks ah pretty ahbitary about things like akridge and such.

> They tell about a man who wanted to divide his fahm between his two sons. He sat at his kitchen table drawing a map and then got up and started pacing off the boundary from the edge of the kitchen table. He went right out the kitchen door to a large oak tree in his pasture, and that line became the sons' boundary. Everything went fine until one day someone moved the kitchen table and then a storm brought down the oak tree. The family's been feuding over that line ever since.

Akaydee-ah Pahk Down East that draws tourists the way ripe bait draws flies. We like to keep an eye on our tourists, and it's a lot easier to do when they're all together in a lahge group. The rule is, when their wallets are empty and their roof racks are full they have to go home.

Akt'n What them show-people from New Yahk come up here summahs to do for those ahty people from New Yahk who also come up here summahs and fill Maine's quaint summah theaters. Makes you wonder why the aktahs and ahty types don't just save all that gas money and stay down there in New Yahk.

Alewife Has nothing to do with either "ale" or "wives"; it's a herring that likes to run upriver in the spring to spawn. You won't find many wives even these days willing to do that. Years ago, folks would catch alewives by the bushel basket and sell them to lobstermen for bait (see below). Some people like to smoke them. But ain't they some difficult to light?

An-day   First name of Maine's beloved artist Andrew Wyeth of Cushin'. In midcoast Maine all you need say is "An-day" and folks just know who you're talking about. The same is true for An-day's son Jay-may. As much as we like An-Day's and Jay-may's paintins, we've been hoping over the years that they'd both soak up enough Down East culcha so as to staht painting up some real aht-like portraits of people like Elvis and Willy Nelson on that fancy black velvet. Now that's ahht. Maybe then they could staht sellin their stuff at WalMart and Reny's.

'newatee   Once he sees he's got enugh for his beeah and his sigretts a rural Mainah at a Mom & Pop store then buys as many Megabucks tickets as he can affahd and the clehrk will ask if he wants "cash" or "'newitee" as if it makes a difference to the poor sap buyin the worthless tickets. See also: Lottree.

Anteeks   Used stuff that summah complaints discovered in Maine houses years ago and started buyin' and stuffin' into theah fancy station wagons—Volvos, mostly—to haul home to New Yawk and Massachusetts. The difference between a valuable anteek and piece of junk depends a lot on whether you're the seller or the sellee.

ANTEEK

Antennah Metal strukcha you set atop a wobbly makeshift towah theah 'side your double-wide trailah for your CB radio transmittin and your 220-channel programmable skannah. Between your CB and ya' skannah you'll be the first one in your part of town to know that there ain't nawthin' goin on no wheah.

Apruhl One of the months near the tail end of the Maine wintah. Once Apruhl arrives in Maine you just know there cahn't be but two or three more months of cold weathah. In Maine Apruhl also means the end of mud season.

Awghst Height of tourist season. Most motels put their No Vacancy signs on toward the end of July and they'll stay on right through Labor Day. In Awghst we might have warm sunny days and beautiful nights or fog thicker than three-in-a-bed along with heavy rain from one end of the month to the other. Thing about Awghst is it likes to surprise you—and it will.

Aya Line If you see a road sign in Brewer that says Air Line you might think it's directing you to the Bangor International Airport (BIA)—but it isn't. The Aya Line is a road that got its name from its bein so hilly it's almost like flyin in an unruly ayaplane. At least that's what they claim. It was built through the woods between Brewer and Calais as an alternate to the coastal road that was well traveled and safer but took a whole lot longer. Innkeepers and other businesses on the coastal route were so concerned about the economic threat of the new route that they made up all kinds wild stories about Aya Line wolves and highwaymen. If you hear a good story as to why it's called the Aya Line, would you let us know?

AYA LINE

Aya Maine has some of the sweetest smellin aya in the country, unless you happen to be downwind of a sahdeen packin' plant, a papah compnee, or a pig fahm. Speaking of aya and its smell—years ago children in the midcoast area sometimes jumped rope to the ditty: "Camden by the sea, Rockland by the smell, Thomaston's a good or town, and Warren's gone to Hell."

Ayuh When you hear "Aloha" you right off think of Hawaii. When you hear "Shalom" you think of Israel. When you hear a crude, vulgar expletive you look around for a Massachusetts drivah. In the same way when you hear "ayuh" you think of Down East. Although many tourists have tried, none has succeeded in pronouncing the word correctly. If you heah the word "ayah" pronounced awkwardly here in Maine, chances ah there'll be a camera-totin', Bahmudah shawts–wearin', *New Yawk Times*–readin outah statah in Berkinstocks and sun glahsses in the vacin'ty.

B

Bah A bah in Maine is a stretch of sand in the water—the kind of formation that gave Bah Hahbah its name. We're told in other states it can also be someplace where folks go to do their serious drinkin'. In Maine most folks have to drink at home, in the bahn, or at a friend's house—if they have any friends. The only known bahs in Maine are said to be in the majah cities of Portland and Bangor. Rumor has it that Lewiston has a bah but—like I said—it's only a rumah.

ROWWF ROWWF ROWWF

BAHK

Bahbah Before talk-show hosts our bahbahs served the same function. They were the wisest people around. Unlike most talk-show hosts bahbahs have at least learned a useful trade.

Bahk All kinds of meanings heah in Maine. On land it refers to the skin of a tree. On the watah it refers to a type of vessel. Bahk is also what you don't evah want your neighbor's dog doin', 'speshlee when you're trying to get some sleep.

Bahkah Loud-mouthed fellahs at the county fairs that do their best to get you to spend all your hard-earned money trying to win some worthless item for your wife or girlfriend—maybe both!

Bahn'kle Cussed little white devils that cling in great numbers to lobstah traps, buoys, and other geah. The worst bahn'kles are the ones on our lovely stone beaches.

Bahtah Tray-din. You want to ruin a tax collector's day, just mention the word bahtah. The idea of tradin items without the use of cash or traceable checks just gives the average tax collector a case of the hives. Here in Maine it's common to trade so much firewood for so many bales of hay; a boat and trailer for a pickup; or a CB for a skannah.

Bait Herring, smelts, ocean perch, and other fish used in catching lobsters or fish. *See also* **Sewshee.**

Bankah Not just folks who loan you money once you prove you don't need it; here in Maine a bankah is what they call a commercial fishing vessel that fishes out to Georges or the Grand Banks and is mostly owned by those othah bankahs.

Baxtah A 300,000-akah (if you're into such foolishness as akahs, see above) state pahk in nawthin Maine named after Percival Baxter, a fahmah guvnah and the fella who donated all the land. Folks in Baahston have their Fenway Pahk; we Mainahs have our Baxtah State Pahk, and that's just the way we like it.

Beach Mainahs figure if you've got 30 or 40 running feet of mostly sand anywhere on the shore you've got all the beach you'll evah need. Any more than that and you're bound to attract too much attention. Oh sure, we have Old Orchard Beach and Popham—but they're the exception that proves our rule. We're also aware that way down south in York County there's a place called York Beach, but hey, no one's perfect. Visitors should know that here in northern New England we're more famous for our rugged, rocky coastline, not our miles and miles of white sandy beaches.

Beam Widest part of a ship. Because of Maine's long maritime tradition such words as beam are often heard in everyday speech describing people or objects other than ships. Although no one would ever say something as insensitive in these enlightened times, in years gone by you might hear a Mainer observe, "Ain't that woman got some beam to her?"

Bean Maine authah Caroline Chute gave us the Beans of Egypt, Maine; Leon Leonwood gave us the Beans of Freeport, Maine; and churches and fire departments across the state have given us the Baked Bean Suppahs of Maine. Many organizations are supported throughout the year with the proceeds from their bean suppahs held at the height of tourist season. A lot of the money needed to get Maine families through the winter comes from folks who work at L. L. Bean. (Most of the other money needed to support families in the state comes from summah complaints, or tourists.)

MAINE CUISINE

BLUE·BRIES

BAKED BEAN SUPPAH

BURGOO

PEEZ

Bench Meetin' place outside many country stores where gossip is exchanged and lies are told.

Bilge That part of a vessel that's below the floorboards and can be a collecting place for some pretty rank water. For that reason the word "bilge" is also used Down East to describe other smelly things like campaign speeches and cah commercials.

Bill-bored Here in Maine there are no poisonous snakes or billboards. People say drivin along Maine roads they get bored because all they see is the trees. Years ago the legis-lay-cha passed a law banning all billboards. When all the bill-boreds were taken down Mainers were surprised to see just how many trees we really do have around here.

Bin-go Populah prayah service held regularly by devout gamblahs in the basement of many Maine churches. Those who can't make it to a church's Sunday service will go out of their way to attend the church's special bingo service. A seculah version of bingo is held for non-believers in many Legion halls throughout Maine.

Bizn'ss Although things look pretty prosperous in southern Maine these days there are pahts of Maine where business is still pretty slow. A store owner Down East told us the other day that his bizn'ss had gotten so bad even the people who didn't pay had stopped buyin'.

Blowin' What the wind does to make the watah on the bay choppee. Because Maine has over three thousand miles of coastline, more than half the state lives within a few miles of the water, so you'll often hear nautical terms like "blowin'." When the wind is over 25 mph and the chop is up to a few feet with whitecaps and the ocean swell is over ten feet, you'll hear a Mainer say something like, "She's blowin' a mite out there s'mahnin."

Boe-din A college in Brunswick named after a fellah with the same name.

Boe-din-ham Maine town named after a college in Brunswick. There is no Boe-din-ham College, although many think there should be!

Bondo The main paht of many Maine cahs. This cherished substance is to Maine what steel is to Pittsburgh—come to think of it, Bondo has replaced a lot of Pittsburgh steel. Without Bondo, half the cars in Maine would be little more than piles of rust. Instead, these cahs are piles of rust held together with bailin' wire and Bondo.

Bottom When you hear someone using the word "bottom" you might think it's a polite way of referring to a part of the human anatomy. But when a Mainer uses the term "bottom," he's mor'n likely referring to the ocean floor. To refer to that part of the human anatomy, a Mainer would say "backside" or "ahss end."

Bowlin' When folks in Maine talk about bowlin', they're more'n like-ly talking about candlepin—the only type of bowlin' officially recog-nized here in Maine. Oh sure, there are a few of those foreign tenpin lanes here and there and even an occasional duckpin lane, but if you want to bowl like a Mainer bowls, deeah, you've gotta go with the candlepins.

Bown-dray The place where one piece of property is supposed to end and another supposedly begins. When we used to ask fahtha how fah back our land went, he'd always say, "Back to that tree line, somewhah." He didn't know exactly where. Fact is, he didn't kay-ah. Now, your out-a-statahs—they care.

Brahpt Mainers are thought be curt in their speech. Some Mainers are even named Curt—short for Curtis. Anyway, Mainers believe you should never say a word that cahn't improve on silence. For that reason folks from away sometimes call us brahpt or shawt. If a tourist should ask, "Is this the road to South Hiram?" a typical Mainer would answer with a brahpt or shawt answer, "No" or "Yes" or "Could be." A long-winded or chatty Mainer might answer, "You know, that's a very good question, but the truth is, I have no idea where that road there goes to."

Brush You want to know what brush is, just let your back field go for a year or two and you'll find out, chummy. That brush will pop up faster than tourists at a yahd sale. *See also* **Puckerbrush**.

Buay Used by lobstermen to mark where their traps are and by the Coast Guard as navigational aids. Often they'll put a bell on a buay to warn where the rocks are. Although it's true that mariners like to know where all the rocks are, they'd prefer to know where they ain't. Also, lobstermen use floats, called buays, made of cedar or styrofoam to hold up their pot warp. *See* **Warp**.

If you walk into a waterfront restaurant and they've got the words "Buoys" and "Gulls" on the bathroom doors, it means they're doing everything they can to distract your attention from their mediocre food and high prices. Expect these same restaurants to have gift shops featuring authentic Maine souvenirs made in Indonesia.

Buht Next to guns, dogs, pickups, traylahs, satellite dishes, CBs, and ATVs, one of the most beloved objects in Maine. There used to be more buhts than people here in Maine, which probably isn't saying much. In summah, folks coming up the turnpike haul at least a few hundred thousand more buhts into Maine every weekend. Buhts, like people, come in all shapes and sizes—from punts, skiffs, dinghies and tenders to skows, yawls, draggers, freightahs, and tankahs.

A newspaper in Maine once ran a personal ad that read, "Single woman with new boat and trailer seeks good man for companionship and possible relationship. All replies answered." A good Maine man replied, "I'm a single man and would be interested in relationship. Please send picture of boat."

Burgoo Time was when the word "burgoo" referred to oatmeal or porridge. These days, if you hear the word burgoo at all, the person using it will most likely be referring to any kind of thick stew. For that reason you might also hear someone say, "That fog is rolling in thicker'n a bowl of burgoo."

Bush hog *See* **Mowin'.**

C

Cah-liss A town on the U.S.-Canadian border in Washington County across the river from St. Stephen, New Brunswick. We don't know how many out-a-statahs have stopped on Route 1 somewhere around Ellsworth and asked someone, "Is this the road to Cah-LAY? and were greeted with a blank stare. You want to ask for Cah-liss or don't bother asking.

Cah Lobstermen's containahs that float and are full of lobstahs. Otherwise, a small, unsuitable vehicle driven mostly by out-a-statahs and some unfortunate Mainers forced to drive one while they save up for the more traditional Maine vehicle, a four-wheel-drive pickup with heavy-duty plow package, running lights, CB, and power take-off.

Cahn't miss it Phrase used Down East when giving directions to summah complaints. Loosely translated, it means, "Ain't no way in hell you'll ever find this place, mistah." Directions Down East can also included phrases like, "At where the old Nelson place used to stand you take a right; or maybe a left, don't hold me to the details." Or "On your left you'll come to the Hupper place—big white house with green trim, big red bahn out back, blue Chevy in the front yahd, a few hosses grazin in a pasture right theah next to the house. Once you see it, you don't pay no attention to it—you keep goin' right on by."

Camden One of the towns mentioned in the jump-rope ditty, "Camden by the sea, Rockland by the smell, Thomaston's a good ol' town, and Warren's gone to Hell."

Camp What folks from away call their summer house a Mainer calls his camp. Mainers believe you should never use two words where one word will do just fine, thank you. Mainers also believe the taxes on something called a camp are likely to be less than the taxes on something as pompous-sounding as a "summer house". A camp is also a place owned by well-to-do out-of-staters and operated for rich out-of-staters who need a place to put their kids while they go on vacation in the Hamptons or on the Cape.

Can'dah Ouwah naybahs. Of all the countries in all the world we could've had for a naybah, we sure lucked out when those Canadians moved in next door. Only time they get a little rowdee is around Victoria Day sometime in May. And don't head for Can'dah in early July, because they don't have Fourth of July up there like we do. We hear they go right from the third to the fifth—of scotch.

Caulkin' If the *Titanic* had been a Maine·built boat with oak planks and Maine-made caulkin', she'd probably have bounced off that ice-berg and would be floatin' to this day. Caulkin' involved taking strips of oakum and spun cotton and with the use of special tools tapping the caulkin' between the planks of a boat. Mostly it worked pretty well.

CB The first talk-radio stations in Maine were CB or Citizen Band radios. CB radios are still a source of information, entertainment, and sometimes even scandal in rural Maine. Years ago along the Interstate, friendly-sounding ladies of the evening used to invite truckers over for coffee, and many innocent Mainers used to think, "Aren't they some friendly?" Weren't they some shocked to learn what those truckers were having with their coffee.

Chainsaw The chainsaw is to rural Mainers what the rifle is to the Marines. If you don't know what that means, go ask a Marine. Come to think of it, rifles are pretty important to rural Mainers, too. On the other hand, we don't exactly know how important chainsaws are to Marines. Anyway, the chain-saw is used in rural Maine for all the obvious things: clear-ing land, cutting firewood, getting racoons out of trees. But here in Maine chainsaws have what some might call novel uses, like fileting those large fish you hear about in Maine fish stories, or carving a wooden Indian out of a tree trunk. No Maine fair is com-plete without at least one chainsaw ahtist.

MAINE AHTIST

Charactah After getting directions from someone in a small Maine town, a tourist said to the native, "Quite a few colorful characters around here, aren't there?" and the native said, "Ayuh, there are. But they'll all be gone by L'bah Day." Tourists might consider some Maine residents "characters," and the residents often feel the same about some tourists.

Chayah After a long, hard day in the fields or the woods or on the water, everyone in Maine likes to have a comfortable chayah to sit in —preferably a reclinah with genuine leatherette covering and a wideenough armrest for your essentials—that would include your dinnah, your beeah and your r'mote.

Chester Greenwood Day Celebrated each year in Farmington, which is Chester Greenwood's hometown. Who was Chester Greenwood? The one for whom Chester Greenwood Day is named, of course. *See also* **Eah muffs.**

Chick'n-of·the-sea A sailah who stays in port when it gets to blowin' and gets a bit choppy outside.

Chips You have your potato chips and your fish and chips, which are common in Maine. But here in Maine we also have cow chips and wood chips—which are as important to Maine's economy in their own way as those other varieties.

Chowdah Whether it's a fish, clam, or corn chowdah, it makes one of the most popular meals in Maine. It took the invention of the woodstove to raise the fish chowdah to a true work of aht. On that woodstove you throw your fish—head and all—in a pot and let it simmer slowly all day. Come suppahtime, you've got yourself a chowdah you could walk across if you had to.

Chum Chopped-up bait. Also a close friend who may or may not smell like chopped bait.

Church Although Maine is not known as a center of religious fervor, still, a Maine town of any consequence will have several churches. You'll have your Congregational or your Methodist (seldom both), your Presbyterian, and then your half-dozen or so Baptist churches. Depending on how many skeptical types there are in town, you might also have a Unitarian church. A Unitarian, of course, is some-one who has given up religion but just can't get out of the habit of going to church—or to church suppahs.

They tell the story about the Unitarian who went shoppin to buy his wife a nightgown. When the clerk asked what size, the Unitarian said, "She's a size 8 but I'd like a size 18." When the clerk asked why he wanted one so large, the Unitarian replied, "We Unitarians would rather search than find."

Church Suppah Some have the notion that all church suppahs are created equal and feature some of the finest dishes served any-where in the State of Maine. Such fuzzy thinking can get you into real trouble, mistah. It might even get you a plate of fuzzy food, now that we mention it. Fact is, you don't want to go near a church sup-pah that someone you have faith in hasn't attested to—in writing if possible. There are as many good suppahs as bad in Maine—you just have to watch out. If you want to try and judge for yourself, the best way to do it is by smell. If you stand outside the church hall and it smells like you're downwind of a Russian fish trawler in mid-July, it's a good bet you should avoid that suppah and go somewhere else. We suppose the same might be true of some restaurants. You might want to do the "Russian trawler" test outside them, too.

Cittay There are only 22 cittays here in the State of Maine and the largest one, Portland, has just barely 65,000 people, so we don't know that much about what folks from away call cittay life, and that's just the way we like it. See **Town**.

Clam The excuse they give for havin' the annual Yarmouth Clam Festival.

Clambake Not for the timid or the microwave crowd. Quite a complicated affair that takes more than a teaspoonful of brains to get right. First, you build a fire over rocks; then when it is burned down, you sweep away the hot embers and lay your clams and fish and lobsters and sweet corn on the heated rocks in beds of seaweed. It's a lot of work, but no one who's ever done it right has ever regretted all the aggravation. Your tourist friends will be some impressed.

Clammin' The act of diggin' a mess of clams.

Close'nuff Mainers don't like to gloat or show off. So if you have a carpenter over to your place doing some finish work and he does a square-cut on a nice piece of molding that's within 1/256 of an inch of being a perfect fit, your Maine carpenter will look it over and quietly say, "Close'nuff."

Coastah We're not talkin' here of something you put under your glass of iced tea, deeah. A coastah in Maine is a commercial sailin' vessel used for haulin' cahgo along the coast.

Cohd The fish that fed the Indians for centuries and eventually brought the first Europeans to these rocky shores in great numbers. It can also be a pile of wood. A regular cohd is supposed to be four feet high by four feet wide by eight feet long, or about 128 cubic feet. There's also something called a "face cohd," which can be four feet high, eight feet long, and almost any width.

Col-bay College in Waterville.

Countree Any place that's a little quieter and a little more out-of-the-way than where you happen to live. If the houses on your road are three miles apart, then someone who lives on a road where the houses are five miles or more apart lives in the countree. We knew some folks who lived twelve miles down a dirt road and their nearest neighbor was about eighteen miles away, but when they went to their camp up to Moosehead, they always said, "We're going to the countree."

The County There are sixteen counties in our state but only one—Aroostook—is known as The County. Kinda like New York bein' known as The City—except folks in Aroostook County have a lot more room to spread out than the poor folks down there in New York. Aroostook is also the only county in Maine to have a war named after it—the Aroostook War—a border dispute with our

Canadian neighbors. If you've nevah heard of the Aroostook War, don't feel bad. It wasn't much of a war since there was only one casualty, and that was some poor fella who was accidently run over by an army supply wagon. It was all settled with the signing of the Webster-Ashburton Treaty of 1842.

Cow puncher A Maine veterinarian. We'd a' never known about this phrase if it weren't for our grandfather who used to tell stories about the cow punchers of Maine. "We had cow punchers Down East long before there were longhorns out west," he'd say. A cow puncher is a vet so-called because of the practice of giving a cow a good punch in the stomach to release trapped gas caused by eating rotten apples or fermented grain. Come to think of it, they could problee use a good cowpuncher down to the Elks Club when some of them fellas get into the fermented grains.

CRUNCHAH

Crunchah Lahge deah. During hunting season if you hear someone say, "He got himself a real crunchah," it means somebody'll be eatin' deah meat for a while.

Cunnin' Something that is wicked cute—like a baby—is called cunnin'. If a Mainah looks into your baby carriage and says "Cunnin," it's a compliment. If they say, "You cahn't deny that one," they're just makin' polite conversation.

Cupsuptic It sounds like the kind of word your plumber would use while trying to explain why your bill is so high. "Not only did we roto-root your drains, but we had to drain and completely reroute your cupsuptic system and then aerate it." In fact, Cupsuptic is a lake near Mooselookmeguntic, which itself sounds like the noise made when the Heimlich manuver is administered to a Mainah who's swallowed a chunk of moose meal.

CUNNIN'

Cutlah A picturesque little harbah Down East that was the home of the world's largest radio station—a one-million-watt giant that dwarfed your big-time stations like WOR and WABC down there in New York. Cutlah Hahbah's radio station was owned by the U.S. Navy. Although it didn't play any danceable music, at least it didn't have any annoying commercials.

D

D'versty A Baptist and a Catholic having coffee togethah at the local dinah. Now, if a Baptist and a Presbeterian go have a beeah together —that would be called "ecumenical."

D'vinin'rawd A tree branch you hold in your hands so you'll look like you know what you're doin' as you stumble around your property wondering where the heck to drill for water.

Daow No. This is probably about as emphatic a negative as you're gonna get along the coast. In Maine courts the word "daow" is always recognized as a negative response, but it may not always work in other juristictions unless you have this reference book with you to show the judge.

Daw-ray A double-ended workboat used for hauling herring nets and such. The daw-ray is confusing to some tourists who learned that the bow is the "pointy-end" of a vessel. When they see a daw-ray—with two pointy-ends—they can't tell if it's coming or going. But that's a tourist for you.

Daw-yahd That paht of your yahd that's by your back daw. Daw-yahds are traditionally the place a Mainer stores those special things he cahn't quite fit in the house but just cahn't beah to paht with right off— things like engine blocks, wood stoves, old tires, chainsaws, couches, boats, moorings, or washahs and dryahs.

DAW-YAHD

Speaking of daws, if you spend much time in Maine you'll notice that Mainahs nevah—and I mean nevah—use their front daw, except maybe in case of a fire or a wake they might be havin' in the front pahlah, and sometimes not even then. The surest way to let a Mainah know you're from away is to walk up and knock on his front daw.

Deah The deah was invented to give Mainers some time off in the fall. Most think the point of deah-hunting season is so Mainers can get themselves a deah for their freezah. Many hunters don't care to get a deah at all, but just like to go up to their camp and have some time off. Getting a deah could only ruin the fun because then you have to field-dress it, tote it out to the truck, load it in, drive it home, skin it, butcher it, wrap it, and freeze it. You might as well be at work if you're gonna have all that aggravation.

Also, term of endearment, as in, "How are you today, deah?" It can be used by two people who have no romantic relationship of any kind. For that reason you shouldn't be surprised or startled if you hear two grizzled old Maine fishermen using the term when referring to each other. And if a clerk in a store comes up to you and says, "Can I help you, deah?" you're not being hit on. Down East the word "deah" has no other meaning—as far as we can tell from here—than "friend."

Del'kasee Any food that's elegant.

Desert of Maine Sounds as foolish as the Sahara Ocean but there really is a Desert of Maine. It's more a marvel of marketing than of geography, though. When this fahm stahted getting all sandy, the folks who owned it said, "Let's sell the livestock and chickens, staht callin our place the Desert of Maine, and chahge people to come look at it. We'll add a snack bah and gift shop and the whole works." They say the family was never that fond of fahming in the first place. One way to tell if someone is a native or transplant is to ask them if they've ever been to the Desert of Maine. Last time anyone checked, no native had evah been theah.

Dickah To arrive at a price through offers and counteroffers. Also, to haggle—usually at a yahd sale or flea mahket—over the price of a worthless item. "He was askin' a fayah price for the Elvis ash tray, but I refused t' buy it because he refused to dickah. It just takes all the fun out of a yahd sale."

Diggin' two-tides When the tide is right and there's enough sunlight on a particular day so's you can go diggin' clams or worms at low watah around six in the morning and then go back again around suppah time and dig yourself some more.

Dinnah Your noon meal—and main meal of the day. For some reason, folks from away eat their dinnahs when most Mainers are havin' suppah. If you're from away and invite a Mainer to dinnah make sure you specify the time because he or she'll likely show up at noon for a dinnah date.

Dite A little bit. "Would you like some milk in your coffee?" "Just a dite."

Dog fish Fish with the worst traits of both dogs and fish, and the curse of the coastal fisherman. They arrive in summah and begin feastin' on haddock somethin' awful—somethin' like tourists, now that we mention it.

Down East   Uppah nor'east paht of the Maine coast. Few people these days know why a place that far north is referred to as Down East. Fewer still can tell you exactly where Down East begins. In Portland they'll insist you're not Down East til you get beyond Bahth; in Bahth you'll be told to go at least to Rockland; in Rockland they'll laugh and tell you to keep going because you won't even get a whiff of Down East 'til you're beyond Belfahst, where folks will insist you've got to get east of Ellsworth, and on it'll go until you get to West Quoddy Head, where you'll scratch your head and wonder, as many have wondered before you, why the easternmost point of land in the United States is called West Quoddy Head.

Dressin'   When you hear Mainers talk about dressin', they're generally not referring to what they put on their salads. More than likely, the dressin' refers to cow dressin' or hen dressin'. Dressin' is used for fertilizer on your garden .

A Down East farmah was talking to his out-of-state neighbor about his strawberries and said, "I've always liked a good hen dressin' on my strawberries," to which his neighbor replied, "I still prefer whipped cream on mine."

Drown-did Expired from taking on too much wahtah.

Dry-go Commonly spelled Dirigo but almost always pronounced Dry-go—it is not the name of a drive-through laundry but is the one-word motto of the State of Maine. *Dirigo* is Latin for "I lead." For registered Maine guides it could mean "I lead people into the woods"; for mariners it could mean "I lead people out to sea." For the average Mainer it might mean "I'd like to lead a bunch of tourists across the Piscataqua River Bridge and tell them to stay there."

Dull The way small Maine towns were designed to be. They say there was a small town Down East so dull that one day the tide went out and never came back.

Dump The original recycling centers. There are houses and trailers that would be bare today if not for some creative dump-pickin'. In years past, dumps were also cultural centers where people met to socialize and look over informal displays of items for possible reuse. When town dumps were in their heyday here in Maine, folks would bring a truck-load of old stuff to the dump, throw it over the edge, and then stand around looking for useful things like old clothes, dishes, tubs, refrigerators, and stereos to haul home and store in the daw-yahd until they might be needed. Most folks in those enlightened times would end up hauling away more stuff than they brought in the first place.

Dyet Most Mainers along the coast tend to have a lot of seafood in their dyet. Some eat so much seafood their stomachs start to rise and fall with the tide.

E

Eah muffs An ear cover invented here in Maine by Chester Greenwood. It's not the kind of thing people in other places spend a lot of time thinking about, but in Maine where the temperature in winter can dip to twenty below for days at a time the eah muff is pretty special.

Eastah Late winter holiday that in other parts of the country is supposed to have something to do with spring. Here in Maine it often comes in the middle of **Mud Season.**

Eel ruht You've heard of the town that was so dull that one day the tide went out and nevah came back? Well, that town here in Maine would be known as an eel ruht—a town so small that at low tide its channels look like the ruhts left by eels going through the mud. We're talkin' a pretty small town here, folks.

Ernin' The money made from werkin'. "He's ernin' a good livin' this wintah trappin' rabbits and beavah."

Earthenware What a Mainah would call a "crock," some fancy shop-owners call "earthenware." You hear a word like this, you know you're in a fancy, high-clahss tourist trap along the coast, full of funny-talkin summah complaints. Just hold onto your wallet and don't give anyone your credit card number or expiration date and you'll be fine. Rather than buy earthenware, a Mainer will wait for that nice grocery-store crockery to go on sale down to the Red & White and snap that stuff up for practically nuthin'. You won't feel bad if you drop that stuff off the table and break it, eitha.

E'gr't A fisherman in feathers instead of boots. Might sound peculiar when you say it that way, but the e'gr't is a species of heron known and grudgingly admired along the coast as the world's greatest fisherman. When you first hear the word e'gr't spoken by a Mainah you might think the person is clearing their throat. In some cases they might be.

Elahkush'n A funny way of sayin' someone talks funny. Also an attempt by some teachers to impose a funny way of talkin' on students here in Maine.

Elekshun Maine elekshuns used to be mere formalities when we were known as one of the most Republican states in the country. During the Presidential race beween Richard Nixon and John Kennedy they were counting the ballots in a small, staunchly Republican town Down East when they came across a ballot mahked "Kennedy." They thought it odd but put the ballot aside, anyway. When they got to the bottom of the pile they came across another ballot mahked "Kennedy" and Ed Beal the Second Selectman said, "Why the s'n-va-b'tch voted twice." So they ripped up both ballots.

El'vaytah Time was the only el'vaytahs in Maine were in the shoes of short men. If you wanted to ride the other kind you had to go clear to Boston. Even now the tallest building in the state is probably no more than twenty stories. We figure there's no need sending a building soaring into the sky when there's plenty of land here in Maine to spread your building out instead of up.

Embahk No passenger vessel "leaves" a place here in Maine, it "embahks." Just so's you'll know—the word has nothin' to do with skinnin' a tree.

Evzdrop From the old Maine habit of listening to people talkin' from the crawl space above the kitchen or pahlah. These days people from away in expensive out-a-state outfits and expensive foreign cameras hanging all over them will often try to blend into the regular crowd down at the local dinah and listen in—or evzdrop—on what the locals are talking about. Fact is, if they understood the language bettah, they'd discover that the locals are talking about them.

Exsentrik A modern ahtist who wants folks to know just by lookin' at him what he does. Because we've had so many aht colonies over the years we've become used to folks known as exsentriks, who usually wear funny foreign-looking clothes and drive funnier foreign-looking cahs. Come summah it's hard to tell one exsentrik ahtist from another because those exsentriks all dress pretty much the same.

EXSENTRIK AHTIST

F

Factree Where your sahdeens and your blue'bries are canned. Time was when many coastal towns from Rockland to Eastport had factrees and most of them canned either sahdeens or blue'bries. And don't believe the people who tell you not to visit a factree if you like sahdeens or blue'bries. The experience may leave you a tad squeamish but eventually—after a year or two—you'll be right back to eating sahdeens and blue'bries like you always did.

Fah Opposite of neeah. But depending on how much you don't want to go there it could be just down the hall.

Fahm Acres of rocky ground surrounded by stone walls where some Mainahs have tried for centuries without much success to grow cash crops like peas, beans, potatoes, and corn, but mostly grow more stones. In time they go broke and sell the farm to a lawyer from Boston.

> A Maine farmer once won $2 million in the Megabucks drawing, and when asked what he was going to do with the money, he said, "I'll probably keep fahmin until it's all gone."

Fahthah What wives in families with children call their husbands—when they are bein' polite.

Fawg Nature's clevah way of drivin' tourists into gift shops and mawls. Along Maine's three thousand miles of coastline fawg can roll in quickah and thickah then almost anywhere else in the world.

FAHM

The Fawks Spot on the Kennebec Rivah where rahfting trips begin.

Fawth of Jewlie Although celebrated across the nation, this national holiday is always a special time in Maine. Because it comes just when tourists begin streaming into the state in great numbers, many Maine towns along Route 1 like to have a little fun with our summah visitors by blocking off their Main Streets for a few hours with their annual Fawth of Jewlie Parade. The town of Wiscasset is famous for this. They have been known to create lines of traffic that stretch all the way south to the traffic circle in Portsmouth, NH. If you're caught in one of these parade lines, just shut off your cah and go watch the parade.

FAWTH OF JEWLIE

Fay-yah An annual event held in most counties throughout Maine where fahm folks bring their animals and crops together for judging. Some of the most exciting times ever held in the State of Maine have been held at county fay-yahs. We won't get into gory details because, well, this isn't the place to get into such descriptions. Fay-yah can also mean "some good." If you hear a Mainah say, "That there's a fay-yah fish chowdah," he most likely means it's the best fish chowdah he ever ate.

Fest'val A word you put after any event here in Maine just to make it sound more impressive than it is. Here in Maine our wintahs are so long we try to have as much fun as we can come summah, so we have a fest'val for just about anything you can name. Yarmouth has its Clam Fest'val; in Belfast it's the Broiler Fest'val; Houlton and Fort Fairfield both have Potato Fest'vals; Rockland has its Lobster Fest'-val; Pittsfield didn't want to be left out so they hatched an idea for an annual Egg Fest'val; Machias has a Blueberry Fest'val; South Berwick has a Strawberry Fest'val; and in Oxford they have what's called a Beanhole Bean Fest'val—we can't explain it here, you'll just have to go see for yourself. By the way, if you have any ideas for other fest'vals, don't keep'um to yourself. We'd like to hear 'um.

Fiddlehead Come spring, you wanna go lookin' for fiddleheads— the shoots of the ostrich fern that are curled just like the head of a fiddle. If you're not sure of what you're lookin' for, you best buy them from someone who does. If you buy them at the right time they're pretty fair eatin'.

Fie-yah Depahtment Depending on the town, the fie-yah depahtment could be a highly trained fie-yah-fitin' force or a bunch of guys who manage to extinguish the fie-yah just before the granite foundation is consumed by flames.

Fir-low Enlightened practice at the State Prison in Warren where cons are occasionally let out so they can go home for a weekend of R & R.

I once went to dinner at a friend's house, and in the middle of dinner we heard several gunshots. When I asked my host what the shots might be about he casually said, "Oh, that's just the Bartlett brothers home on fir-low from Warren. They came home last night, got right down to drinking. Been drinking all day today and now they're playing with their guns."

"Drinking? Guns? That can't be part of their firlow agreement," I said.

"Well, why don't you go over there and tell them that?" said my friend.

"No, I don't want to tell them," I said.

"No one else does either," said my friend.

Floundah Don't think stumble, think sole as in filet of. The floundah is an elegant Maine fish that comes in many varieties, like yellowtail, gray sole, blackbacks, dabs, and sand floundah.

Free range To folks from away, free range has something to do with chickens that are let out to run around the yard instead of being penned up. In Maine free range means a fairly decent stove you found at the dump. See also **Dump.**

Frenchie Another name for a Franco-American. Years ago a Portland radio station created a broo-ha-ha (which in French, we think, would be "le hulla-balloo") with a character known as "Frenchie." The Frenchie character was stereotypical (which meant he typically spoke in both bass and treble ranges) and was played by someone who was himself Franco-American. After eight years on the air, Southern Maine's Franco-American community finally decided that enough was enough (or is it un'oeuf?). Anyway, Frenchie had to go. After trying to add a little balance with stereotypes of an Irishman, a Jew, and an African American, the station decided just to shut up and play music.

Friggin' Fooling with. A church deacon was once overheard saying something like, "I wish the pastah would hurry up and get here so we can get the meeting underway and staht friggin' with the numbers in next year's budget." Here the word friggin' obviously means to deal with or fuss with. Now, if the deacon had said, "I wish that pastah would get here so we can get this friggin' meetin underway," that might be considered improper.

G

Gahd'n A fenced-off area reserved for weeds. Despite our short growin' season some Mainahs try real hahd to put in a gahd'n to get a little taste of fresh vegetables and put some by for wintah. What most get is a nice patch of weeds.

Gamy Nothin to do with baseball or cahds. When a deer tastes gamy it means it wasn't dressed right. Anything that's a bit foul around the edges or you can smell downwind for some distance is also called gamy. You might hear a Mainer say, "When those five fellas from New Jersey finally left that hunting camp up there on the ridge that they'd been staying in for over a week, didn't it smell gamy."

Gawmy If you heard a Mainer say, "That President Gerald Ford, my, isn't he some gawmy?" would you know what he was saying? No? In that case I'll tell you—gawmy is clumsy, awkward, gawky, or ungainly. Some might want add the word "lumbering" to the list, but here in Maine we have a high regard for the lumbering profession.

Get your bait back A catch at least as big as the bait used to catch it. If you go buy a bushel of ocean perch for lobstering, you hope to get back a lot more than a bushel of lobster. When someone uses a lot of bait to get a small mess of fish it's said, "He barely got his bait back." We've heard the expression used in describing a smaller than average baby. "You see Hollis's new baby? He barely got his bait back on that one."

Gettin' by Payin' most of your bills. In pahts of rural Maine people have been known to list gettin' by as their "occupation" when fillin out official forms.

Glooskap This is not an item found in your L. L. Bean catalog—although, now that we think of it, it would make a good name for some hunting apparel. In fact Glooskap was a hero-god of Maine's native Americans. Glooskap lived on the summit of Mount Katahdin.

Godfrey (also **Godfrey Daniel**) In better mannered times Godfrey was used in place of the Lord's name by people who wouldn't use the Lord's name in vain, and "Godfrey Daniel" in place of "Gosh Darn."

Gore Has nothin' to do with President Clinton's Vice President, which, depending on your politics, you might find a good thing. Here in Maine a gore is a piece of land left over from what some might consider sloppy surveying. They say when Maine was being laid out some surveyors were using true north as a reference point and some were using magnetic north. What was left over from all this surveying was called a gore. Over the years most of these gores—like Prout's Gore in Freeport, for example—have been absorbed by nearby towns. But you'll still find places on Maine's map like Coburn Gore and Misery Gore—you'll just have to look hard to find them.

Grahss about the bow A new beard that looks like a boat that's been in the water too long and had grahss groing on its bow. Some think the expression refers to the practice of smuggling contraband or what's known Down East as whacky-terbacky in the bow hold of your boat. When hippies came to Maine in the 1970s in great numbers the expression was revived and can still be heard in stores along the coast.

Grange Every town in Maine that's been around for a while will have itself a Grange hall. The Grange movement came to Maine around 1873 and has had its ups and downs. These days they say it's mostly down. In some Maine Grange halls you'll find entertainment, suppahs, auctions, flea mahkets, and such. In others you won't find much of anything.

Guess prob'ly If the parking lot at the store in town is overflowing with out-a-state cahs and you can barely get in the place, you might hear one Mainer say, "Looks like the summah c'mplaints are back in force." And the other Mainer might respond, "I guess prob'ly."

Gull When not flying around dumps a gull spends its time perched on a lobster boat; and don't that irritate the lobsterman. Also known as sea gulls, gray-backed gulls, or Arctic (black-backed) gulls, gulls nest on offshore islands and spend their days flying around wharves and messing up boats. Be careful, because they've also been known to drop s'prises on inattentive tourists.

> A couple from the midwest was watching a flock of gulls outside a waterfront restaurant when one made a deposit on the husband's head. The wife said, "Stand right there, dear. I'll get some toilet paper in the restaurant." A nearby fisherman said: "No point doing that, lady. By the time you get back, that gull's gonna be halfway across the harbor."

Gunwales The top plank on a vessel. Even though it's spelled gunwales, you don't want to go up to a lobsterman at some dock and show off by saying something like, "So, how's the gunwales on your boat, there?" That's because the word is pronounced gunn'ls. If you hear a Mainah say, "When she left the cove and headed for Rockland she was filled right to the gunn'ls with sahdeens," it means she barely had a plank a' freeboard. Somewhere in your travels you also might hear someone say, "I was just down to the Tru-Valu and they's having quite a sale on house paint, so I filled my pickup right up to the gunn'ls with about fifty gallons of the stuff—even though I don't have anything I can think of that needs painting right at the moment. But I tell ya, as soon as something starts peeling up there to my place, by gory, I'll be ready for it."

Gurry If you've ever looked at a commercial fishing boat or fishing gear spread along a dock somewhere and wondered what all that gunk was all over it, then wonder no more. The stuff you were looking at is called gurry.

Gurrybutt First of all, it has nothing to do with the backside of anything. A gurrybutt is any kind of receptacle put on the table for your lobster and clamshells. You might not hear the word in those fancy Portland restaurants but "lobster-in-the-rough" places Down East will often place one on the table and say simply, "Here's your gurrybutt."

GURRYBUTT

Gut Slight indentation in the coast shaped like the gut of a fish. A gut just barely serves as a hahbah or ankorage. The picturesque village of Port Clyde in Knox County was always known to early fishermen as Herring Gut. When summer complaints began buying up cottages in the area and writing home to their friends in Boston, New York, and Philadelphia, they didn't like it a bit that they had to put Herring Gut, Maine, as their return address. So they started a move to change the village's name. But to many locals it will always be known fondly as Herring Gut.

H

Harbor master In most coastal towns the harbor master is like the last kid picked for the baseball team when you're choosin' sides. If someone wants to hold some office in the town, the selectmen will say, "OK, Hollis, you can be our habah mastah." A harbor master is supposed look after the harbor and enforce any rules the town might have that affect the harbor. A harbor master will also assign moorings and keep the peace where needed.

When a friend of ours—who lacked any nautical experience to speak of—was named harbor master of a well-known Down East harbor, we called to congratulate him and said we were curious how he ever ended up with the job. He said he had been the assistant harbor master when the harbor master quit. When we asked why he quit, our friend said, "Because someone threatened to shoot him." That should give you an idea of the kind of job it is in some of Maine's more contentious ports.

Hardscrabble Because we're blessed here in Maine with lots of rocky soil, most every town has a Hardscrabble Road. When the from-away crowd starting arriving in Maine in great numbers in the 1970s, many of them objected to living on something called Hardscrabble Road, so they joined with some of the more genteel locals and managed to have the names of many of Maine's Hardscrabble Roads changed.

Hawd Used for hawling clams-known as a clam hawd. Folks from New Jersey think we're saying something is difficult—as in "I can't do that, it's too hawd." Come to think of it, filling a clam hawd these days can be pretty hawd.

Haywire Also called bailing wire. Time was when everyone who had cows and horses around their place had all kinds of haywire or bailing wire. We had neighbors who managed to keep most of their mechanical devices held together with haywire, Bondo, and a few wads of chewing gum. These days, with fewer livestock around, people have turned to duct tape.

Heirship property When a batch of far-flung relatives have a claim on a piece of land, it's called heirship property. In order to tidy up the deed some lawyer has to draw up legal papers and have every one of those far-flung relatives sign off on whatever claim he or she has to the tangled property. Depending on how many relatives there are and how much time and money you're willing to waste, you might be able to straighten things out in one lifetime.

Hi watah High tide.

Howse Mainers seldom refer to their dwelling as their howse but as their place. A howse is the enclosed area around the wheel of a lobster boat. The typical Maine place is divided into several pahts: you've got your kitchen, your dyn-in room, your back room, your front pahlah, your sun room, your side porch, your down sulla, your up-attick, your el.

I

I'lund More than just a piece of land surrounded by wahtah. To know what an i'lund really is you gotta go live on one for a year. Then you'll find out.

I'talian The official state sandwich—the classic Maine I'talian—is a lot more Maine than it is I'talian. The first I'talian-style sandwiches were made in Portland around the turn of the century for shipyard workers of all races, religions, and creeds. They became so popular that before long almost every sandwich shop in Maine had some version of the I'talian sandwich. Sons and daughters of Italy from other parts of the country may dispute the name I'talian, since many of Maine's classic I'talians are made with such ingredients as American cheese and Oscar Mayer bologna, but no one can dispute the popularity of Maine's classic I'talian.

J

Jack To go out at night and shine a strong light directly into the eyes of some poor woods critter for the purpose of shooting it. It's considered socially unacceptable in Maine.

Jackson Lab Home of one of the largest collections of rodents in the world. You may not read about it in any of the glossy tourist brochures but this lab in Bah Hahbah is a mouse metropolis; it also houses hamsters and other experimental rodents. They're all bred by Jackson Laboratory, the renowned cancer research facility.

Jag A full truckload of firewood. Few people can eyeball a pile of wood and say, "Ayuh, that there's a cord all right." For that reason most serious wood buyers in Maine—where wood-buying is still a very serious business—like to buy their wood by the truckload. When a truck is loaded right to the gunn'ls, so that one more stick would go sliding off—that's what's called a jag a' wood.

Jam On a Maine farm it's what you make with some of your apples, blueberries, raspberries, and such. On a Maine river, a jam was a real mess, with too many logs piling up in too small a place.

Ja'pan For quite some time now this Asian country has been Maine's best seafood customer. They even buy our bait. See **Sew'shee.**

Jeezly A youneekly Maine word that can be used as adjective or adverb. "That Ed Tuttle on the Board of Selectmen is so jeezly contrary I can't figure out how he ever got elected." Or, "They're serving those jeezly small pancakes down to the dinah this morning." It's one of those Maine words that if you have to ask what it means it's clear you shouldn't be using it.

Jet ski A floatin' snowm'beel used in wahm weathah.

Jonesport We're not exactly sure what to say about Jonesport, but it just doesn't seem right to have a book about Down East Maine words that doesn't say something about Jonesport.

Jordun Mahsh Famous Mainah. When you hear the name Jordun Mahsh, you probably think of the famous department store in downtown Boston. Fact is, that store was founded by native son Eben Jordan from Danville, Maine.

K

Kahfee Some places they like their kahfee strong and their women weak. In Maine we like them both pretty rugged. Some diners up country have kahfee strong enough to seal your driveway. The kawfee in other diners is so strong it might do permanent damage to your driveway—to say nothing of your insides. Our doctor says if we cared that much about our insides we wouldn't be drinking coffee in the first place. He's no fun. A notorious restaurant along the coast dumped their old kawfee out the back door for years and that land is now a Superfund site.

K'tahdin Mount K'tahdin—an impressive 5,267 feet of granite.

Ken'bunk'puht Back in the 1980s and early 1990s when George Bush Senior was Vice President and then President it was bumpah-to-bumpah through Ken'bunk'puht and clear out through Ocean Drive. And it was not just your wealthy Cadillac- and Lincoln-drivin' Republicans, either. Every two hundred cars or so you'd see someone in a Peugeot who just had to be a Democrat, and they'd be drivin' out there to see the Bush place, too.

Kee-osk Fancy little glahss-enclosed bull'tin boards where out-a-statahs find out about things like fancy shops, bowteeks, and trenday restaurants. You'll nevah see a good yahd sale or flea mahk't on no keeosk, we can tell you that right now.

KEN·BUNK·PUHT
RUSTICATOR

Kulcha What a lot of summah people go lookin' for as soon as they arrive in Maine for their vacation.

Kwi-ah Church singers. Some kwi-ahs can be pleasant to listen to; others can produce a sound that would scare the hell right out of most any believer.

L

Labah Day A Maine device used to get rid of tourists. The way we heard the story, a group of Mainers were looking for a way to remind the summah complaints that it was time to pack up and go home, so they come up with the idea of Labor Day. The firm rule was that by Labor Day your boat was to be hauled out of the water, your pipes were to be drained, your camp closed, and you and the wife and kids were supposed to be on the turnpike heading south. No excuses. The idea worked slicker than a smelt for several decades, but then the summah people—just like mosquitoes and black flies—started staying longer every season.

Lake A body of fresh water that is not a pond or a bog. When people from away see a decent-sized body of fresh water here in Maine that might be called something like Papoose Pond, they say, "Back home that would be a good-sized lake." Maybe so. But here in Maine we have—at last count—around 2,500 lakes and ponds that cover about one million acres—give or take a square foot or two—and we still don't have a hard and fast rule on what constitutes one or the other, lake or pond. If you've got any ideas on the subject, we'd like to hear 'um.

Landin' My grandfather used to talk about the landin' or p'blic landin' like it was the center of town. He and his family lived out on a small island, so they'd have to come into the landin' every morning to go to school.

Lahff What people from away think Mainahs are too unemotional to do. But if a Mainer pushes himself, he can go way out there beyond a smile, and eventually find himself lahffin. A crowd down to the Grange hall sat though an evening of Maine humah, and when it was finally over a man turned to his wife and said, "That fella was so funny I had all could do to keep from lahffin'."

Ledge-i-slaycha As individuals they're fairly decent folks. But put 'um all together up there to the state capital in Augusta and let 'um sit as lawmakers and they proceed to get into all kinds of mischief. And it don't make any difference whether you're talking about the House or the Senate. If one body starts some mischief, the other body has been known to pick it up and carry it a little further. A recent Ledge-i-slaycha passed a bill naming a certain type of dirt the official soil of the State of Maine. Now, you'd think that politicians—bein' in the public eye and all—would be a little squeamish about the subject of "dirt," but there they were passing a bill about it.

Liyuz' Convenshun Any gathering of two or more Maine storytellers. To encourage such conventions some Maine towns have what are called liyuz' benches in their general store where stories—hence lies—are told.

Lee The side of the vessel you always want to empty your buckets on unless you want the contents to come right back at ya. All settlements on Maine islands are on the lee side of the island. You see someone emptying a bucket to windward and chances are they haven't spent too much time at sea. It's not something a person of average intelligence does more than once, we know that much.

Lite-house At one time these beacons of the coast were pretty important for navigation. But these days—what with your Loran or global positioning equipment and all—lighthouses are only used as backdrops for vacation photos.

Lottree Way back in 1823—when Maine was but three years a state—the Legdge-i-slaycha allowed the Cumberland and Oxford Canal Co. to have themselves a lottree to raise money for their canal. We're not sure what the state's cut of this deal was, but we can assume the state treasurer got a hefty share of the action.

Over the years we've had lots of local lottrees to raise money for bridges and public buildings and so on. Then back around 1973 the Legdge-i-slaycha needed more money (When don't they?), but they were squeamish about raising taxes again or trying to come up with one or two more things to tax, so they copied our neighbors to the west and decided we'd also have us a voluntary tax—otherwise known as the lottree. It was the cleverest thing any tax lover ever saw: people would voluntarily come into their local store, they'd voluntarily reach in their pockets and just turn over their hard-earned money to the clerk who at the time would be acting as agent for the state during this voluntary tax transaction. Oh sure, the Legdge-i-slaycha realized it had to sweeten the deal a little by makin' folks think they had some chance of winning more money than they ever dreamed possible, but that was a small price to pay. The people loved it and the state's coffers were filled with these voluntary donations.

Lobstah Known in scientific circles as *homarus americanus* (which they claim is Latin for humorous American—I guess because those sophisticated European cousins of ours thought it was pretty funny that anyone in their right mind would even think of eating such an unappetizing-looking creature) the lobster can hold its own when put up against the tastiest foods on the planet—like snails and sturgeon eggs. It makes little difference whether you serve your lobster boiled, baked, stuffed or stewed, sautéed, saladed, or Newburged—you'll find your lobster makes mighty good eating.

Lobster trap Years ago lobster traps were made of wooden laths, and when tourists found them along the shore, they thought they were quaint and took to tying them to their cars and taking them home to make coffee tables. They were called "conversation pieces," although I can't imagine the conversation they might start. Now that most lobster traps are made of coated wire mesh, they look like green shopping carts without wheels. Let's see you start a conversation with that.

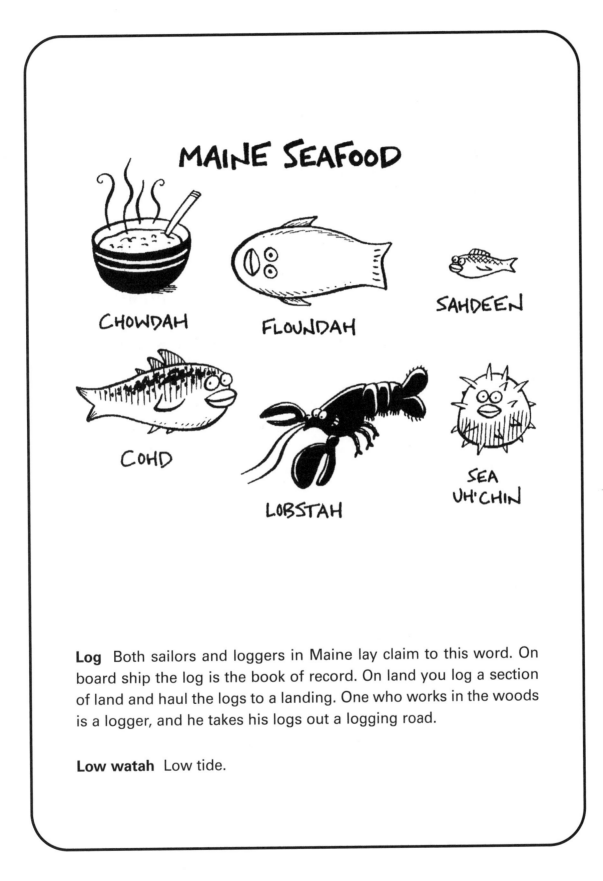

MAINE SEAFOOD

CHOWDAH

FLOUNDAH

SAHDEEN

COHD

LOBSTAH

SEA UH'CHIN

Log Both sailors and loggers in Maine lay claim to this word. On board ship the log is the book of record. On land you log a section of land and haul the logs to a landing. One who works in the woods is a logger, and he takes his logs out a logging road.

Low watah Low tide.

M

Maine What's it mean? Where'd the name come from? We'll do our best to explain. On some of the first maps of New England—which were printed and distributed by the Colonial version of AAA, and included the area we now know and love as Maine—in the spot where Maine was, the map maker wrote "The Main Land." Then a few years later the king granted a charter to Sir Fernando Gorges (pronounced "gorgeous") and Captain John Mason (pronounced "mason"), both of the Royal Navy. In the space on the charter form where it asks, "So, what'chu blokes gonna call this chunk of land of yours?" these two old sea dogs wrote in the word "Maine." Trouble is no one ever bothered to ask either Mason or Gorges, "Why Maine?" If they did ask, no one ever bothered to record their answer for posterity. So even though we know there's a place called Maine in France and we hear there are Maines in Virginia, Ireland, and even in the Orkney Islands, we're not sure—nor do we care a whole lot—if our state is named for any of them.

Mahgr't Affectionate name for Maine's beloved Margaret Chase Smith of Skowhegan, who served for many years in both the U.S. House and Senate.

Mahssachusetts A southern state (or commonwealth, as they insist on calling it) that Maine has always had a testy relationship with, even in good times. For a couple hundred years Maine was owned by this southern commonwealth, until we managed to wrestle ourselves loose and become an independent state in 1820. Things went pretty well between us for over 150 years until the folks from Mahssachusetts decided they didn't like the deal any more. Do you know—they've been buying our state back one house-lot at a time ever since.

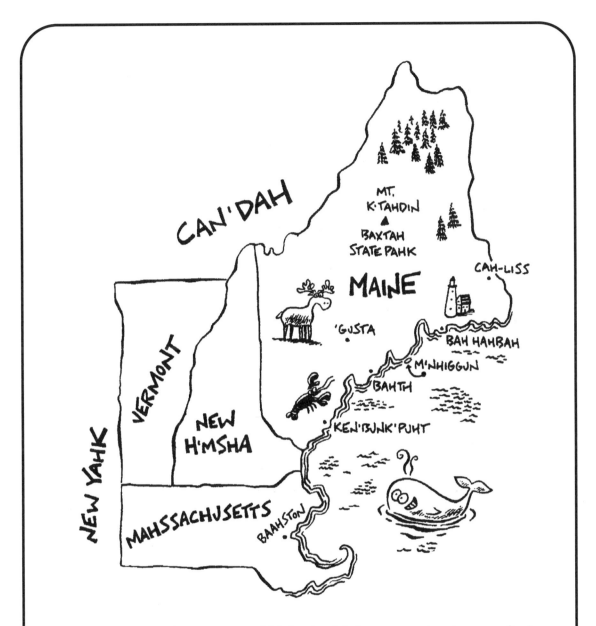

Mawll Place where many of Maine's old downtown businesses fled to, hoping to find customers. What they found were high rents, so many are now fleeing creditors.

Meddybemps You have to want to get there awful bad to find yourself in this colorful Washington County town on the Air Line between Brewer and Calais. Sometimes referred to as "Muddy bumps."

Mess There's a whole mess of meanings to this word. You might hear a Mainer say: "While I clean up this mess in the kitchen, you go down to the shore and dig us a mess of clams for supper; but be careful not to get caught clamming without a license or you'll find yourself in some nice mess."

Mill On the coast more than likely it's a trap mill—a place where laths are milled for lobster traps—although that's not done so much any more since lobstermen went over to wire traps. Inland more than likely it's a paper mill. If you can't bear to be downwind of it after a few whiffs, then more'n likely it's a paper mill.

Moose If a camel is a horse designed by a committee, then you might say a moose is a deer designed by a committee that's been drinking heavily. The moose was once endangered here in Maine but has made an impressive comeback. There are so many around now that we are even allowed to hunt them. You first have to enter a moose-hunt lottery, and if you're one of the lucky ones you get to go up north and shoot yourself a moose—which in some cases is about as difficult as hitting the side of your barn with a high-powered rifle from about twenty paces. Once you shoot the moose then the real fun begins. First you have to field-dress your 900-pound prize, and then you and your friends have to haul it out to your truck and over to the tagging station.

Moosehead The name of Maine's largest lake. Moosehead is about 35 miles long and 10 miles wide—give or take a foot or two either way. They say if you do the math that comes out to about 120 square miles. If they had a lake like Moosehead in, say, Rhode Island, you wouldn't have room for much of anything else, including the mayor of Providence, but you'd have some awful good fishin'.

M'nhiggun First time we ever saw a beatnik was on the *Laura B.* dock in Port Clyde. The *Laura B.* was the boat that took folks to M'nhiggun—an island about 11 miles out in the Gulf of Maine. Almost from the begining M'nhiggun has been a gathering place for ahtists. These days—come summah—M'nhiggun is just crawlin with your ahtists and folks who like to hang around ahtists. It gets so bad out there you wonder how them ahtists evah get any of their aht work done.

M'NHIGGUN I'LUND

Moo-vahs and **Shay-kahs** We hear that in some places moo-vahs and shay-kahs are big shots with all kinds of influence. Here in Maine we don't generally lump the two together. A moo-vah is someone who owns a truck and moves people's furniture from one house to another. And shay-kahs are members of a small religous community up there to Sabbathday Lake.

Mowah Although we don't have anywhere near as many fields in Maine as we did a hundred years ago, we still have enough, and all of them have to be mowed. For that reason Maine has all kinds of mowahs.

Mowin What's done to fields to keep them from becoming pucker-brush.

Muskie Another famous Mainah. In some places when people hear the word muskie they think fish. Here in Maine when we hear the word muskie we think Ed. Ed Muskie was a legislator, governor, U.S. senator, and Jimmy Carter's Secretary of State.

Mussel When folks in Maine talk about a mussel beach, they're not likely talking about that showy place out in California. A mussel beach in Maine is a good place to get yourself a mess of mussels for suppah.

Muthah A husband with kids will often call his wife muthah—as if the wife needs another kid to deal with. See also **Fahthah.**

N

New H'msha We go back a long way with our neighbors to the west. Of all the contiguous 48 states in the Union, Maine is the only one that shares a border with only one other state. Of all those other states we could have had as neighbors, somehow we ended up with The Granite State. They had one of the nation's first lot-trees, they have no income or sales tax, they get all that national publicity every four years with their first-in-the-nation primary, and we get to watch it all here next door in Maine.

> Years ago, during a border dispute, surveyors were going up the line trying to straighten things out when they discovered that a farm owned by Thurland White was actually in New Hampshire instead of Maine as was previously thought. So the surveyors went up to Thurland's house and told him that his farm wasn't in Maine at all but was really in New Hampshire. It was reported that he said, "Well, thank the Good Lord Almighty, because I don't think I could have stood another Maine winter."

Nor'easter A pretty bad storm no matter what it's called. These days most people can't remember whether a nor'easter means the winds are coming from the northeast (nor'east) or the winds are heading to the northeast. In case you're one of those people, you should know it don't make a whole lot of difference where the winds are coming from or going to—if you hear the word nor'easter in a weather report it means a pretty bad storm is on its way and there's likely to be a lot of rain or snow and coastal damage. Most boats and lobster traps are hauled out before a nor'easter just to be on the safe side. See **Sou'wester.**

Nay-cha What tourists will drive thousands of miles to "see" and "experience" here in Maine. It's because of the cold winds of nay-cha that Mainers spend a lot of time cutting wood, buying sump pumps (to protect their cellars from the floods of nature), getting themselves good moorings to protect themselves from the high winds of nature, and buying themselves bug zappers so they can sit in the dark in the backyard in summer and send a few thousand volts of electricity through the pesky bugs of nature.

No'wayah When a Mainer uses the pronoun "she," more'n likely he's talking about a boat. So if you get a Mainer to help you get a mooring to secure your new boat, he'll go up the quarry and get a two-ton granite slab. Then he'll have a hole drilled in the slab and he'll have a steel ring bolted on to it. Then he'll go buy fifty feet of two-inch galvanized chain and about thirty feet of one-inch nylon rope. Next he'll have the granite, chain, and rope moved into place at low tide with a work scow. Then he'll fasten your boat to the mooring with the rope. When he's all done, he'll stand there on the bow and say, "They-ah. She wun go no'wayah." And she wun, neither.

Nun buoy This word has nothing to do with the member of a religous order, although the shape of a nun buoy does kinda resemble the general shape of a nun in a traditional habit. The nun buoy is a navigational aid to mark a channel or keep vessels from going onto a ledge.

O

Old Orchard Beach No one knows how it happened. We're still trying to figure it out. After the glacier was finished carving out the rocky coast of Maine, it dumped a few million yards of sand down south of Scarborough, and all that sand eventually became Old Orchard Beach. But it all worked out for the best. All those people who can't stand to look at picturesque fishing villages, and instead need crowds of people and lots of shops selling greasy fried dough, vulgar T-shirts and overpriced gifts, as well as a few honky-tonk bars and discos and overpriced seaside motels, can head for Old Orchard Beach and go nuts. We don't have to worry about offending anyone down there with this book, because as far as we know there's not a bookstore in the town. Besides that, there's nothing in this book vulgar enough to put on one of their T-shirts.

O'laydee Not an Irish surname but what some might consider a disrespectful name for a wife or girlfriend—sometimes both. In some social circles you might hear a man say, "I'd like to go see my o'laydee but I don't want the o'laydee to know about it."

One-lunger Not a lifelong smoker just back from surgery, but a one-cylinder, two-cycle engine used Down East years ago—when lobstermen went from oars to motors.

P

Paintah When someone in Maine tells you they're a paintah, it could mean they paint houses or boats, or they could be one of those ahtists that paint on canvas. We're not suggestin' that house paintahs and boat paintahs aren't ahtists, it's just that you'd never get one of those fellas to call himself an ahtist, but if you've ever seen one of them paint a waterline on an 80-foot yacht, you'll know what we're talking about.

Paul Bunyan No matter what you've heard over the years about Paul Bunyan and Minnesota, you should know that the legendary lumberjack was born right here in the State o' Maine. The City of Bangor—once the lumber capital of the world—commissioned a famous ahtist to make them a giant statue of Paul which still stands today—or at least was still standing the last time we checked.

Paypah Principal product of Maine's wood products industry, made possible by our vast woodlands. Paypah mills pay some of the highest wages earned in the state, but you wouldn't want to live downwind of one. Also a publication that, if local, can be a source of news. A Mainer once observed, "We don't buy the paypah to see what's going on. We already know that. We buy the paypah to see who's gettin caught at it." In some towns the local paypah is the best place to keep a secret. You take something you don't want anyone else to know and you put it in the paypah, and no one will ever see it.

PAYPAH

Peavey The Peavey is a tool—a pole with a funny metal doohickey on the end—used for rolling logs. It was invented by a fella named Joseph Peavey, a blacksmith from Bangor. Peaveys got a real workout during Maine's legendary river drives when loggers would use their peaveys to keep the logs from jamming. Our legislature outlawed river drives in the 1970s, but they said it was still OK to own and operate a peavey.

Peat Not Pete but Peat. You may not know it to look at us, but Maine has massive amounts of peat—what with our hundreds and hundreds of bogs and heaths. Peat is vegetable matter that has decomposed in water. You can burn it for heat like they do in some countries or you can use it in horticulture.

Peez One of the first items planted each year in many Maine gardens. More than any other vegetation grown in Maine the lowly pea is the most talked-about and argued-about plant grown in Maine. Some of my earliest recollections involve hearing folks argue down at the store about the planting of peez. Religion and politics pale as topics of animated discussion when compared to the lowly pea. Most arguments involve when to plant your peez, what variety to plant, and how long before your peez are ready to eat. Some gardeners have been known to use small sticks of dynamite to get their seeds in the ground long before the ground is thawed and ready. Others will wait until Memorial Day weekend to plant. Once peez are planted, members of both camps will follow the progress of the other's peez—like they were dealing in military intelligence. Regardless of who plants when, both camps like to dine on fresh, homegrown peez and fresh-caught Atlantic salmon on the Fourth of July.

Pew A favorite place in Maine for Sunday naps.

Pickup Vehicle of choice Down East, where people can be pretty clever in their use. A deputy sheriff was on the rise overlooking a town when he saw a fella in a pickup going along loaded with chicken cages. A quarter-mile down the road the fella got out of the cab, took a two-b'-four from behind his seat, walked to the back of the truck, and began pounding like a mad man on the chicken cages. The chickens went crazy. Soon the fella got back in the truck, drove another quarter-mile, and repeated the same pounding business. Some curious, the deputy came up behind the fella and pulled him over. He said, "As far as I can see, you're not doing anything illegal, but why do you keep stopping to pound on them chicken cages?"

"Officer," the man said, "I've only got a half-ton pickup and I'm trying to carry a ton of chickens, so I've got to keep half them chickens in the air at all times."

Pine Tree What the longhorn is to Texas, the mighty white pine is to Maine.

Pirates Companies that operate service areas on the turnpike aren't the first pirates to show up in Maine. Pirates of the swashbuckling variety like Samuel Bellamy and Captain Kidd himself operated here in the state.

Place No matter whose name is on your deed, your piece of property—or place—can be known by the name of people you never even met who owned it years ago. You might tell someone in town where you live and they'll say, "Oh sure, the old Nelson place." Confused, you might say, "Well, I don't know anything about the Nelsons. We bought the place off the Strouts." And he'll say, "That's right. The Strouts owned the Nelson place for years and years. They bought it off the Leightons who bought it off the Cutlers who bought it from the Browns. Now, it was the Browns who bought it from the Nelsons." No one can explain how a place gets its name or why the name doesn't change when the house is sold to folks with a different name. It just doesn't. Whatever you do, don't try and change the name of your place on your own. It'll never work.

They tell the story about a con man from away who was going door-to-door in the Down East town of Milbridge trying to collect funds for a bogus charity. When a woman asked, "So, are you from around here?" he said, "Oh, sure. I'm from STEW-ben, right up the road." Well the woman knew right there the fella couldn't have been from any such place and was lying through his teeth because if he were from around there he'd know the town is called Stew-BEN.

They also tell the story of the couple from Rhode Island who got lost up north and stopped at a store to find out where they were. The husband went in and asked the store owner where the road to the left went and the store owner said "Moosealuk-maguntic." The husband then asked where the road to the left went and the store owner said, "Wittapitloc." So, the husband said what if I took the road that goes straight— where would I end up? The store owner said, "Mattawamqueag." The husband got back in the car and his wife said, "Well, do you know where we are now?" The husband said, "Hell, no. Fella in there doesn't even speak English."

Plantation We're not talkin' cotton or sugar here but woods. Maine has forty-six plantations.

Pond *See* **Lake**. Don't ask why, just go see it.

Pop'lah Could be a tree, or a person who is well liked.

Port Any place to be in a storm. Also, the left side of a vessel—the side with the red running lights. Old salts say a good way to remember what side of the vessel has the red light is to remember that port wine is red; and if you've been drinking too much port wine or the like, you better not be running your vessel anyway.

Potato Maine's largest agricultural crop. A few years ago some members of the ledge-i-slaycha wanted to have a picture of a potato on all Maine license plates, but some lawmakers were afraid that it might be confused with a moose turd. The potato advocates saw no problem with that, but the idea was eventually dropped.

Privy Before indoor plumbing every Maine house had one, usually located on the lee side of the house, so as to be upwind of it as much as possible. Years ago, mischievous youngsters enjoyed tipping over privies on Halloween night.

P'tit M'nan When Samuel de Champlain sailed along the coast of Maine in 1604 he named a lot of places along the way, and some of those names remain—although not necessarily pronounced the way Sam would have pronounced them. Petit Manan (Puh-TEE Ma-NAW) became known Down East as P'tit M'nan.

One morning a father asked his son if, as a prank, he had tipped over the family privy the night before. When the son said he had, the father punished him. The son said, "When George Washington told the truth about chopping down the cherry tree his father didn't punish him, did he?" The father said, "No, but George's father probably wasn't sitting in the cherry tree at the time."

Pro-bishon Long before the rest of the nation went dry, Maine had its own pro-bishon laws. In fact, pro-bishon in the United States was originally known as "the Maine law." Pro-bishon began in Maine in 1851 and lasted 83 years. But with over three thousand miles of coastline and all kinds of cargo vessels coming and going, a few drops of demon rum managed to get into the state all the same.

Pulp In other places the word is used to describe a kind of fiction. Here in Maine pulp is the main ingredient in paper—whether it's your common toilet paper or your fancy coated paper used for printing your big-time news magazines. Some people don't think there is much difference in the end result.

Puckerbrush Any brush growing thick along the side of a Maine road that you can't put a name to.

They tell the story of a tourist who ran into a local fella's pickup and knocked the truck right into the puckerbrush. There was a lawsuit, and months later when the case came to court the tourist arrived with his high-powered defense lawyer who put the local truck driver on the stand and started grilling him. The lawyer said, "When the accident occurred you told the officer at the scene that you were all right. Now—ten months later—you're claiming you were injured. Exactly when did you go from being 'all right' to being 'injured'?" The Mainer said, "When your client knocked my truck into the puckerbrush, I had a cow in the back of that truck and she went sailing into the puckerbrush with it. A state trooper arrived on the scene, saw my cow in the puckerbrush moaning, and said, 'That animal is in misery.' He then took out his revolver and shot the cow dead. Then with his gun still smoking he leans over to me and says—'Now, are you alright?'"

Punt Don't think football, think boat. A punt is a boat with a squared end to the bow—making it hard for some inexperienced people to tell exactly where the bow on a punt is. That can be pretty upsetting, because if you don't know where your bow is you can't tell whether your boat is coming or going. Come to think of it, some people who have never even seen a punt have the same problem.

Puffin What you see colorful old-timers doing on their corncobs outside a Maine country store. Also, the name of a colorful offshore bird sometimes called a sea parrot. Although both the old-timers and the birds are considered colorful, as a rule the old-timers don't dive for fish and the birds don't smoke corncobs.

THE MAINE DICTIONARY

Q

Queen City For reasons we're not even sure we want to know, Bangor is known as the "Queen City". As far as we can determine neither Queen Victoria nor Queen Elizabeth ever set foot in the jewel of the Penobscot, but it's called the Queen City just the same.

Quo-ray A hundred years ago Maine's granite quo-rays were turning out tons and tons of granite that was used to help build many of the major cities on the eastern seaboard. In fact we cut and sold and shipped out so much of our own granite that back in the 1980s when the new Portland Museum of Art wanted some granite in their new building they had to go to Canada to get it. These days those old quo-rays are filled with water. Some are used for swimming and others are used—illegally—to dump old cars.

Quizz'cal You want to get a quizz'cal look you just ask an ol'timer in a small Maine town what people around there do for excitement. He'll probably say something like, "Can't say. I've nevah been excited."

R

Rattlesnake We here in Maine have heard and read about rattlahs and other poisonous snakes, but like Ireland there's not a one to be found anywhere in Maine—unless you count some members of our legal—oh, never mind. Like we said before, we have no poisonous snakes here in Maine.

Rahfting Goin' *down* the creek without a paddle.

Reedempshun C'nt'r Some tourists see signs for one of our bottle reedempshun c'nt'rs and assume they have something to do with one of them zealous religous cults and they start conjuring up all kinds of notions of what might be going on inside. A reedempshun c'nt'r is just a place you bring your empties to get all your nickels back. When we passed the bottle bill here in Maine some years ago, the Mom 'n Pop stores lobbied for reedempshun c'nt'rs so people wouldn't be coming into their little corner store with railroad cars full of bottles.

Reny's What L. L. Bean could be if it were paying attention. Reny's is a department store that has some of the most useful stuff sold anywhere in the State of Maine and it's all under one roof. Folks say if you can walk through a Reny's and not see something you need, then you're just not living right.

Rocks What Maine is made of. What flat is to the Great Plains, rocks are to us, from our rocky shores to our rocky fields and the rock walls that surround them.

Route 1 This important east-coast highway begins right in the northern tip of Maine in Fort Kent and winds its way down the eastern seaboard to Key West, Florida. While passing through Maine it becomes an awful lot of Main Streets. Although the Penobscot is our largest river, Route 1 is also considered an important river of commerce—having more tourist traps per mile than any other road in Maine.

Rugged The coast of Maine is described as "rugged", and so are many other things. In a dinah don't be surprised if someone describes the coffee or the bran muffins as being "a mite 'rugged' this morning."

Rusticator At first you might think this word describes a Maine automobile that has spent too many winters on Maine's salt-covered roads, but the word has nothing to do with rust. A rusticator is someone who comes to Maine in late June and stays pretty much for the whole summer.

RUSTICATOR

S

SAD School Administrative District—made up of several small towns not big enough to support a bloated bureaucracy on their own. SADs were the creation of Augusta politicians who worried that people didn't have enough things to argue about and needed some help.

Say-ins Mainers are known for their say-ins. Tourists will often stop and talk with a Mainer in hopes of hearing a Maine say-in. There was once a couple from little Rhode Island who stopped to talk to an old farmer, and when they asked him what he had learned from his many years of living in the country he said, "Never step in anything soft."

Scouse When times are hard Mainers might serve "scouse"—which is clam chowder without the clams. These days, if a Mainer goes into a seafood restaurant and orders a bowl of clam chowdah, only to discover that no clams were sacrificed in its making, you might hear someone at the table say, "Will you look at the 'scouse' they're serving up in this place? You'd think at these prices they'd at least give us a picture of a clam so's we can remember what they look like."

Scrid If you're serving up a blueberry pie to your Down East neighbor and he or she says, "Oh, just give me a 'scrid,' theyah, deah," they're not mispronouncing a word for fish, but asking you for a small piece of pie—a "dite."

Scrod Any of several different kinds of white fish from the North Atlantic. Scrod might be cod, or it could be haddock, it might be pollock or then again it could be hake. If you see scrod on a menu, chances are it's pollock, hake, or cod—because if the restaurant had gone out and gotten haddock, most likely they'd tell you.

Sea uh'chin To give you an idea of what folks along the coast think of this creature you should know its unofficial name is "whore's egg." In scientific circles it's known as an echinoderm, and it has lots of sharp spines all over it. These days some divers can make a day's pay diving for sea uh'chins, most of which are sold to Japanese customers.

Slectm'n No matter what the selection process, most small Maine towns are run by what is called a Board of Slectm'n and they're known as selectmen regardless of how average they might be.

Seine (pronounced sane) It has nothing to do with your mental state; it's a net for catching herring. When the net is dragged across the mouth of a harbor it's called stop-seining, and when it's in a circle it's called a purse seine. Once the herring are gathered together in a tight place, the fishermen throw a large vacuum hose into the middle of them and suck them up into a trawlah. The herring trawlah brings the catch to the canning factory where the women of the town with still more nets (in their hair) put them into cans. Once in the cans, they're called sahdeens.

S'lf i'mploy'd When you read in the paper that someone is s'lf i'mploy'd it often means they don't really have a job. If it says Mr. Peavey is s'lf i'mploy'd in the marine products industry, it could mean that he digs worms or clams or dives for sea uh'chin. And if he's good at it and works steady it could also mean that he earns more than you do—so don't laugh too loud.

Sewshee In Japan, an appetizer. Down East it's used as bait.

Shagimaw Although we've never seen one ourselves, we've heard enough about them to know that they exist in Maine in some form. According to those who have seen them or at least tracked them, the shagimaw is a four-footed animal with two feet like a moose and two like a bear, so it makes tracks that can be pretty difficult to follow—just ask any out-of-state hunter who has tried to track one. Mainers gave up tracking shagimaws long ago. Now we just tell stories about them.

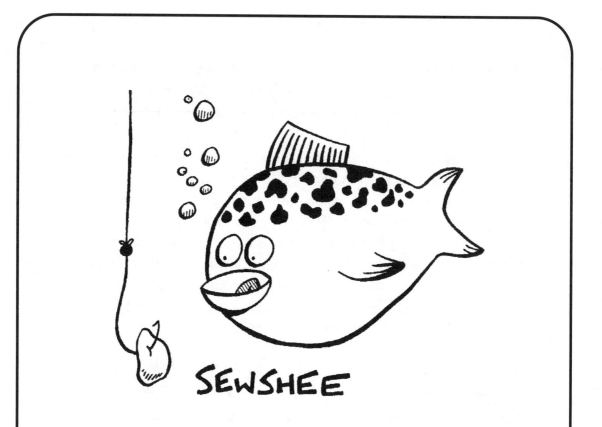

SEWSHEE

Sheddah A naked lobstah that's molted and shed its shell. Sheddahs are known in the market as soft-shell lobsters and are cheapah than hard-shell. For years customers have argued among themselves whether a sheddah is a bahgin because it's cheapah and tastes bettah or is no bahgin 'cause there's less meat to it and it's watery. It's sort of the Down East version of the "tastes great, less filling" argument that goes on among your beer connoisseurs.

Skannah An electronic device for listening in on police, fire, and other emergency calls to see who's gettin' in trouble and who's behavin'. People who own them hate to admit it, but skannahs in Down East Maine only demonstrate how dull those towns really are.

Smelt As in, "Slicker than a smelt."

SHEDDAH

CENSORED

Snow   Like Eskimos, Mainers have dozens of words for snow. Unfortunately, since this book is meant for family reading, we cahnt list any of them here. If you use your imagination, we figure you'll probably come up with a good many of them.

Snowm'beel Jet ski adapted for wintah use. If you intend to have any social life whatsoever in northern Maine in wintah, you bettah get youself a snowm'beel, mistah. What with your snowm'beel clubs and dances and suppahs and trips, you don't want to leave home without one. You wouldn't get very far anyway. What the camel is to your Bedouin or the horse is to your cavalry, the snowm'beel is to your average Mainer. Come winter, when there's five or six feet of snow on the ground, a snowm'beel looks like sensible transportation.

Soup dee jur An item on the menu of many fancy restaurants. No Mainer would ever order the "soup dee jur" because you never know from one day to the next what it's going to be.

Sou'wester Waterproof hat worn by fishermen during, well, during a nor'easter, come to think of it. Don't even ask "Why aren't they called nor'easters?" They're just not! OK?

Speedo It's one of the scariest things you're likely to see on the coast of Maine in the summah. For some reason begining about the first of July large, white walrus-like humans will gather at Old Orchard Beach and strut around by the water in small bathing suits called Speedos. The company who makes these tiny items of clothing has tried on numerous occasions to get cease and desist orders against these beefy individuals, but the frightening ritual continues. Just let this be your official warning.

Stah Famous person from television or movies. Lots of big stahs have homes along the coast of Maine, but I'd have my license to operate as a Mainer taken away if I told you where those houses are. Every once in a while you'll see a stah walking around Freeport or Portland's Old Port or up there on Mount Desert Island. If they get any notice at all, it's usually from some tourist. Mainers figure they came here to Maine to get away from nosey fans so we more or less leave them alone—unless they try to cash a check or something; then we'll ask them for an ID.

Stahbid The right side on a vessel—with the green running lights. Unlike for the port side there are no riddles or old sayings to help remember all this; you'll just have to keep this book handy when you're out to sea, that's all.

Sternman Lobsterman's helper who looks toward the back end or the "stern" of the lobster boat. Once the lobsterman has taken the "keepers" (lobsters big enough to sell) out of the trap, he slides the trap along the gunwhale to the sternman who empties the "shorts" (lobsters too short to sell) out of the trap. He then rebaits the trap and sets it. Come to think of it, the sternman does most of the work on the lobster boat. And just a word of advice—If you're standing on a dock Down East talking to a lobsterman, and at some point he refers to his "sternman," please don't corrct him and say, "Don't you mean 'sternperson'? I can tell you right now—he doesn't. The title is "sternman," regardless of gender.

Stickah Winshield decoration issued by official inspection stations and needed on every Maine cah before it can go out on the road. You could have a cah with a blown engine, bald tires, and no transmission, but if she's got a good stickah that cah is worth something, mistah. Guys with pickups that were total wrecks but had a good stickah have been known to sell the stickahd windshield off the truck for $100.

Stones Along with rocks, boulders, and pebbles, they are an integral part of Maine's landscape, vegetable gardens, and beaches. Unlike other places in the world, here in Maine we have what are called stone beaches. "Who needs sand?" says the gang down at the Chamber of Commerce. We're pretty patient here in Maine, and figure you give nature another few thousand years or so, those stone beaches of ours will be some of the finest sand beaches anywhere. By that time your lower states like Florida and the Carolinas that brag so much about their beaches now will be some fathoms under the Atlantic.

Summah That time, usually in early-to-mid-July, when the weather gets a tad warm during the day and it can even get a dite uncomfortable at night. Summah folks think when it's summah in Massachusetts or Maryland that it might be summah here in Maine, so they arrive with suitcases full of shorts and tank tops only to freeze to death in their rented cabins.

Swiss chaahd Has to be one of the toughest plants grown in Maine. Some insist it's edible, but we can't say one way or the other because we've managed to avoid eatin' it to this point. We do remember that swiss chaahd was always the first item to appear on the chalkboard in front of the vegetable stand in town. It was always a sign that things were starting to grow—but nothing yet that anyone would want to eat.

SUMMAH FOLKS

T

Tah When Maine built large wooden vessels, tah was heated up in great quantities and poured between the planks as a new vessel was built. Tah was eventually used to cover Maine's quaint dirt roads.

Tagging station Where dead deer and moose are tagged during hunting season. It's also the place where some go to tell about the moose that got away.

Tel'phone Sometimes used for communicatin' in place of ya CB radio. Years ago rural Maine had party lines—which had nothing to do with Democrats and Republicans. A party line was eight or ten families hooked up together on the same tel'phone line. While you were talking on your phone you had to assume that there were quite a few of your neighbors on the line listening in. A rural Mainer was once asked in a job interview if he had ever done any public speaking and he said, "Only when I used my tel'phone back home."

TEL'PHONE

Tie-yah Not just used on cahs but also used in some areas as places to plant flowers. Along the shore tie-yahs are used as bumpahs on docks to keep boats from getting banged up. Tie-yahs are also used on the top of some mobile homes to keep the roof from blowing off.

Tips On the coast, what waitresses make in restaurants and house-keepers make in motels. Further up-country tips from fir trees are what folks go hunting for to make Christmas wreaths. Folks in Washington and Hancock Counties "go tipping" come mid-October and return home with truckloads of evergreen tips and boughs.

Tomalley The green part—or liver—of the lobster. Tourists and others from away will often turn up their noses and make all kinds of comments about how disagreeable the tomalley looks, but your average Mainer will just sit quietly and eat it. It's just one more way of telling the away folks from the natives.

Toms'tun Former home of Maine's famed state prison and a poplah tourist stop because of its Prison Shop where items made by prisoners were sold. You could generally tell the sentence of the prisoner by the items he made. Someone in for a short sentence would make something like a pine wall plaque in the shape of the State of Maine. A lifer might have made a model of Notre Dame Cathedral from Ohio Blue Tip wooden matches and Maine toothpicks—all of which had been individually sanded and glued together. Folks in Thomaston used to resent it when their town's name was used to imply that the town was the prison, as in, "He's currently doing 8 to 10 in Thomaston," or when mothers warned their children with threats like, "You better watch your step, young man, or you'll end up in Thomaston like your father and brother."

Toothpick Piece of wood used to pick teeth. You may laugh, but the lowly toothpick is one of Maine's most profitable forest products. Figure it out. A box of toothpicks costs about $1.25. Wholesale, a cord of birch goes for about $80. Do you have any idea how many toothpicks you can make from a cord of birch? A lot, mistah. Not so funny, now, is it?

Tourist season Like black fly season, tourist season begins just when things start to warm up—around mid-June. In order to give summer visitors the idea that maybe it's time to pack up and go home, Mainers invented Labah Day.

Town With a mere 22 cittays and 430 towns, it's a good bet Mainers know a lot more about towns and town life than they do about cittays and cittay life. A town is a place where everyone knows your business, which can be upsetting to some people—especially those who have no clue as to what their business is.

Town man'jah If there is a more thankless job on the face of the earth we've yet to hear about it. No matter what a town man'jah does or neglects to do, he's blamed for anything in town that isn't right. It's not that he has all that much to do. Fact is the town man'jah of the average small Maine town doesn't have much to do at all. Our town man'jah had a sign on his desk that said, "So little time; so little to do."

Transplahnt Plants or people who move from one place to anothah. When used elsewhere the word most always has to do with plants and trees. When used in Maine the word most always refers to a person from away who has moved to Maine. Transplahnts try awful hard to fit in, but most are pretty easy to spot. For example, most transplahnts just can't bring themselves to buy a Ford or Chevy, preferring BMWs and SUVs. And you'd never catch one putting an NRA or even a SAM (Sportsmen's Alliance of Maine) bumper sticker on his car. If you see someone driving around town in a Peugeot and sporting a "Meat is dead" stickah on the back, it's a dead giveaway they're a transplahnt.

TRANSPLAHNT

TRAYLUH

Trayluh You could write a book on this word alone—and when this book here is done maybe we will. As far as many Mainers are concerned, be they evah so humble, traylahs are home. We figure in this wide world, if it's worth anything you should be able to take with you—like to Florida in wintah. That's why so many of us have house trayluhs, boat trayluhs, snowmobile trayluhs, horse trayluhs, and livestock trayluhs. If it's an important part of Maine life, there's a custom trayluh made to haul it. For less important things that don't have a trayluh named after them we have the useful utility trayluh. Lot's of folks in Maine earn livings going from one trayluh to another. They'll wake up in their double-wide and go to work driving a semi-tractor trayluh. They'll come back to their double-wide after eight or ten days on the road, have a quick nap, and then hook up the boat and trayluh to their 4x4 and head up to camp—a log cabin–trayluh combo.

Trowt pond One of the most famous trowt ponds in Maine is right there in L. L. Bean's store in Freeport. Mainahs who always avoided trips to Bean's because of all the tourists—preferring instead to order by catalog—just had to go see that clevah trowt pond for themselves.

U

Unorganized Township Maine has always had a lot more land than people to fill it. And even though we have 432 towns, 22 cities, and 46 plantations, we have a lot of land left over which we call "unorganized townships." They shouldn't be confused with our "disorganized" townships—but I wouldn't want to say in print what towns those might be. Folks who live in 'um know all about it. Just ask.

W

Warp First off, it has nothin to do with our sense of humah. In other places the word "warp" refers to what happens to wood when it's left out in the rain. Oh sure, it's what can happen to a boat's wooden deck if it's left out in the weather too long unprotected. But here in Maine warp is the common term for the rope used to haul lobster traps.

Wahden You wanna see an official Maine wahden? Go fishin' any-whayah in Maine without a license and they'll appeah right out of the fresh Maine aya. The only time I ever met a wahden in the woods was when I was working out of the Ellsworth bureau of the *Bangor Daily News* and so anxious to go fishing one afternoon after work

WAHDEN

that I neglected to go get a fishing license. I figured, "The place I'm going to is so remote no wahden will ever find me there." Well, I had just finished covering myself with fly dope and getting into my waders and into the stream when I heard some branches crackling. A few minutes later a friendly wahden appeared on the shore. After asking how the fishing was he asked if he could see my license—haven't seen a wahden since.

Wahtah Mainahs have a strange relationship with the curious substance called wahtah. Cahn't live with some'vit; cahn't live without the rest. Maine has over three thousand miles of what's called "wahtahfront"—not counting our rivahs, lakes, streams, bogs, and great ponds. If you see wahtah from your front window that's good—your place is worth a lot of money. On the other hand, if you can see wahtah seepin into your cellah after a hard rain, that's bad. Then again if you cahn't find any wahtah in your yahd after drilling for a well that's also bad—it means you're gonna have to haul your watah. 'Course, you might find watah on your place but it's commin down through the roof—and that's not good at all.

MAINE WAHTAH

Winnebago A rolling fat globule that clogs Maine's traffic arteries sumthin awful all summah. What the swallows are to Capistrano so the Winnebago is to the highways of Maine. Now that might not be the best comparison, what with your swallow being a cute little bit of a thing with feathahs and your average Winnebago being an exhaust-belching monster that's a coupla city blocks long and usually has a SUV being towed along behind just for good measure. Point is, like the swallows that return in the spring, the Winnebagos return to Maine in wahm weathah—in great numbers.

Wood stove Not a stove made of wood but an ironclad monster used to burn hahdwood, mostly during cold weathah—which in Maine would be from late Septembah to mid-May.

WHITE WAHTAH RAHFTING

X

X The only word we can think of that starts with X in Maine is the name Xavier, as in Francis Xavier—and it's usually a dead giveaway that the person is Catholic and more'n likely lives in one of Maine's traditional Catholic enclaves—either Portland, Lewiston or Bangor—and went to parochial school.

Y

Yacht Place where summah folks meet to have cocktails or wine—nevah beeah. Also what out-a-statahs call any boat with a cabin, no mattah how small. A Mainah's boat—no mattah how fancy—is nevah called a yacht for the same reason a camp is nevah called a summah house. It just don't sound right. If you hear the word yacht, we'd be willin' to bet a dollar to a duck egg that it's an out-a-statah's boat that's being talked about.

Yankee Many Down Easters of English decent are also called Yankees. When a Mainer calls himself a Yankee, you're safe in assumin' he's not talking about baseball. To be a Maine Yankee is to endure—from birth to death—cold winds and ice and snow in wintah; and black flies, tourists, and the Red Sox in summah.

About the Author

John McDonald began absorbing Maine words and phrases over fifty years ago in Tenants Harbor. Over the years he continued soaking up the distintive inflections of Maine while working as a reporter for the *Bangor Daily News, Portland Press Herald,* and *Lewiston Sun Journal.* These days he performs as a storyteller, writes a syndicated newspaper column, and hosts a popular talk show on WGAN (AM 560) in Portland.

About the Illustrator

Peter Wallace's cartoons on local politics and culture appear regularly in the *Boston Globe.* Born in Rhode Island, he now lives in Arlington, Massachusetts.